IMAGES of America
THE GRAND HAVEN AREA
1860–1960

The Tri-Cities are formed by the municipalities of Grand Haven, Ferrysburg, Spring Lake, and surrounding townships. This spectacular 1960s aerial view, looking east, catches most of the area in one shot.

IMAGES of America
THE GRAND HAVEN AREA
1860–1960

Wallace K. Ewing, Ph.D. and
David H. Seibold, D.D.S.
for the Tri-Cities Historical Museum

ARCADIA
PUBLISHING

Copyright © 2002 by Wallace K. Ewing, Ph.D. and David H. Seibold, D.D.S.
ISBN 978-1-5316-1351-8

Published by Arcadia Publishing
Charleston, South Carolina

Library of Congress Catalog Card Number: 2002106083

For all general information contact Arcadia Publishing at:
Telephone 843-853-2070
Fax 843-853-0044
E-Mail sales@arcadiapublishing.com
For customer service and orders:
Toll-Free 1-888-313-2665

Visit us on the Internet at www.arcadiapublishing.com

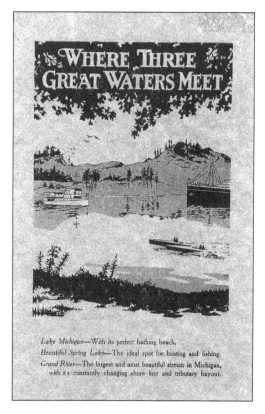

In the mid-1920s, the Chamber of Commerce produced a brochure publicizing the area's resort life. The 28-page booklet highlighted Lake Michigan, Spring Lake, and the Grand River.

Contents

Acknowledgments		6
Introduction		7
1.	Resort Life	9
2.	Life Saving Service and Coast Guard	23
3.	Industries	31
4.	Downtowns	45
5.	Services, Private and Public	61
6.	Residences, Humble and Grand	79
7.	Transportation Over Land and On Water	91
8.	Recreation and Leisure	107
9.	Disasters, Large and Small	121

Acknowledgments

An undertaking such as this one clearly depends upon the combined efforts of a number of people. Fortunately, the Tri-Cities Historical Museum is blessed with a collaborative spirit in both its volunteers and its professional staff. Special thanks go to Jeanette Weiden, Assistant Curator, who laboriously reviewed the Museum's extensive picture files and assisted in the photo selection process. She also provided a helpful perspective by reviewing the collection and making many suggestions that ultimately led to the completion of the project.

We are especially thankful to the hundreds of local citizens who, over a long period of time, have donated their treasured photographs to the Museum. These images help convey what life was like "in the old days" better than words. Special thanks to Jim Benes, Tom Fisher, Chuck Angus, Wally Ewing, and Anton Ebel for sharing their valuable photos. We also extend our appreciation to Dennis Swartout, Executive Director of the Museum, whose support and keen perception kept the project on track and on time.

Wallace K. Ewing, Ph.D.
David Seibold, D.D.S.

Each summer the Coast Guard is recognized by a large celebration that draws people from across the country. The final night of the observance ends with a special program at the Musical Fountain followed by a colorful and dramatic fireworks display.

INTRODUCTION

It is a happy coincidence that the settlement and growth of the Grand Haven area was contemporaneous with the development of photographic techniques. The archives of the Tri-Cities Historical Museum contain hundreds of "snapshots" of places, events, and people from the 1860s through the 1960s. These snapshots provide an invaluable visual glimpse of those people and how and where they lived. More than 200 of those images are collected in this book.

Nestled in wooded dunes and surrounded by the waters of Lake Michigan, Spring Lake, and the Grand River, the village was aptly named Grand Haven. Rix Robinson, a fur trapper and one of the first white men to settle in the Grand River Valley, gave it that definitive name to reflect its position as a large, accommodating, and safe harbor. On a Sunday morning in the fall of 1834, Rev. William Montague Ferry, accompanied by family and friends, sailed into the protected port and called it home. Before long the fledgling lumber industry took advantage of the towering white pines that grew for miles around and used the extensive waterway system to ship milled lumber to Chicago, Milwaukee, and other major cities along the Great Lakes.

By 1890 the seemingly endless tracts of forest were gone. The two dozen sawmills that lined the Grand River had closed or moved to other areas and the area's economic base looked bleak. But within ten years the reputation of Northwest Ottawa County as an outstanding resort center was well established. Some entrepreneurs early on saw profit in developing resorts. The Pomona House in Fruitport, the Spring Lake Hotel, and the Magnetic Mineral Springs Resort in Grand Haven became well known as healthful retreats for believers in the curative powers of the area's magic waters. Similarly, the Highland Park Hotel, rivaling Mackinac Island's Grand Hotel in size and grandeur, afforded visitors a refreshing retreat on the Lake Michigan shoreline. Increased affluence and leisure time allowed thousands of summer visitors to visit these splendid retreats.

At the same time, local business leaders developed plans and financing to attract manufacturing businesses to Grand Haven. Many large factories, employing hundreds of people, responded to the prospects of a good port, an energetic employee base, and tax incentives. The railroad made its first appearance in 1858. By 1900, there was one major line carrying riders up and down the Lake Michigan coast and another that carried goods and people east. Ferry boats made connections with the trains and continued the journey westward to Milwaukee and other sites. At about the same time, an Interurban railway provided fast and inexpensive transportation between Grand Rapids, Spring Lake, and Grand Haven. The decline of the lumber industry was soon forgotten in the context of a burgeoning resort and manufacturing base.

The images selected for this book provide a pictorial history of Grand Haven and its immediate surroundings. They are presented in nine categories: Resorts, the Coast Guard, Industries, Downtowns, Services, Residences, Recreation, Disasters, and Transportation. While the pictures do not capture the area's vast, rich history in its entirety, they do convey a sense of the people, places, and events that made possible today's remarkable community.

One

RESORT LIFE

As the resort business expanded, so did the number of hotels and boarding houses. The Central Hotel, located in the Village of Spring Lake, offered a pleasant place for summer visitors and temporary workers. The plank sidewalk was necessary to protect pedestrians from the muddy, unpaved streets.

In 1871, Willard Sheldon dug a well on the northwest corner of Washington and Third Streets. At a depth of 160 feet, he struck a flow of sparkling water charged with minerals. He soon built Sheldon's Magnetic Mineral Springs Sanatorium on the spot to attract people who wished to "take the waters."

Dwight Cutler was not one to let an opportunity for profit go unclaimed. The Cutler House, a luxurious five-story hotel directly opposite Sheldon's Magnetic Springs, boasted rooms for 300 guests, steam heat, a steam-driven passenger elevator, hot and cold running water, and gaslights.

Grand Haven photographer Nat Brown perfected a system of taking dramatic aerial pictures from a kite. This 1909 shot, looking north, clearly reveals the Highland Park Hotel, several cottages, and the Interurban tracks.

Wearing the latest in fashionable swim wear, this group in front of Boseker's Pavilion at Highland Park enjoys the sandy beach and waters of Lake Michigan. The woolen swim suits were heavy and "itchy" when wet, but the prospect of a day at the beach attracted people of all ages—and still does.

By the early 1900s, boating, swimming, and sunning were popular recreational activities. Highland Park attracted summer visitors both for the day and for a week or more. August Boseker's beach was a popular spot for resorters to rent a woolen bathing suit and enjoy a dip in the water.

In addition to its magnificent hotel and rustic cottages, Highland Park offered a wide beach, warm sands, and the refreshing surf of Lake Michigan. August Boseker bought this building in the early 1900s, repaired it, added bathhouses, added a 200-foot pier, and rented rowboats. It also served as the Interurban station. Today the building houses the Bil-Mar Restaurant.

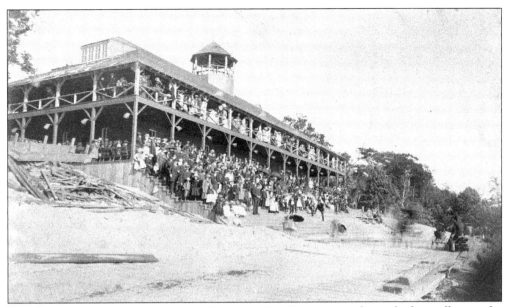

The "bracing" fresh air of the Lake Michigan shoreline attracted people from all over the country. One of the most popular destinations was the elegant Highland Park Hotel. Built around 1890, the two-story frame hotel featured 36 rooms in the main lodge and 15 more in an annex. Porches on both levels extended the full length of the building. The beach was only a few steps away.

The Hyland Gardens building was not only turned to a north-south axis, but it also had many additions to make it suitable for large dances and other kinds of recreation. During the winter, great ice "bergs" formed along the lakefront, providing unique hiking adventures for the local citizens.

Hyland Gardens vibrated to the beat of many big name "swing" bands, such as Charlie Byrd, Gene Krupa, and Tommy Dorsey, as well as local drummer/band leader Sammy Fletcher, Jr., who performed on a regular basis. Guests also could roller skate, bowl, shoot pool, or play ping-pong and shuffle board.

When the Grand Haven State Park opened in 1922, the Interurban still provided service to the area, but the automobile was clearly making an impact. The shape of the roadway within the State Park gave rise to its enduring nickname, the Oval. Lake Avenue appears in the lower right corner.

This aerial view dates back to about 1950. The Swimmers' Pavilion, built in 1937, is in the lower left corner and the Oval Inn is near the center. The entrance to the State Park was then located between the pavilion and the inn. The "Castle" can be seen at the top of Five Mile Hill.

Like Highland Park, the Oval attracted armies of tourists every summer. The wide beach and refreshing waters appealed to people of all ages and from all walks of life, just as it does today.

A stroll on the pier has always been a form of enjoyable, refreshing exercise. Today's hikers might not wear as much clothing as these four people, but perhaps this was a cold day! The catwalk above the two women allowed lighthouse keepers to attend to their duties even in the stormiest weather.

Although not as crowded as it is today, by 1920 a collection of cottages lined the west slope of Five Mile Hill. Summer guests could look out upon a wide beach and the ever changing face of Lake Michigan. Before Harbor Drive was extended to the beachfront in 1922, people arrived here on the Interurban.

Located on Pigeon Creek in Port Sheldon Township, Fridrich's Point Resort opened in 1901. Albert and Lena Hoecker Fridrich of Chicago built the 21-room hotel and several small cottages. Ottawa County purchased the 44-acre parcel in 1998 with the hopes of turning it into a park.

Called Peaceful Retreat, this rural resort offered visitors in the early 1900s a chance to "get away from it all" on 40 acres of gentle hills and shade trees, with access to Spring Lake. The resort later was called Ripple Haven.

In 1887, Jacob and Anna Ferris bought a 70-acre fruit farm and opened the first summer boarding house on Spring Lake. Anna built the large Willows Hotel in 1893, four years after her husband's death. The resort, on the east side of Spring Lake, was one of many that beckoned summer visitors.

Situated near Petty's Bayou on Spring Lake, Prospect Point Manor was built in the late 1800s. In the 1920s, Warren A. Beale ran the resort. It consisted of several large buildings and cottages, and offered a total of 60 rooms that rented for $3.50 a night during the summer season.

A 1930s brochure for Prospect Point Resort advertised, "*Modern Lodge and private Hotel Cottages. Accommodations for 150 guests. Unusual meals . . . private beach . . . golf and tennis nearby . . . shuffleboard . . . motion pictures . . . water sports . . . organized entertainment. Midnight snacks. Select clientele.*"

Entrepreneurs in Spring Lake Village capitalized on the magic waters craze. In 1871, a group of investors constructed four large cottages and a magnificent four-story hotel with 74 rooms. The serene waters of Spring Lake provided excellent boating, but bathing, bowling, and billiards were also available.

Besides the hotel, the Spring Lake House offered guests 30 additional rooms in the adjoining cottages. Visitors could sail, fish, swim, bowl, play billiards, or just relax, as these four gentlemen are doing under the shade trees. The hotel was destroyed by fire in 1916, but the cottages remained into the 1920s.

In the early 1900s, Andy Floto ran the River View Hotel in Grand Haven. Originally called Andres House, it was built in 1874. Riding the crest of the post-World War I popularity of the automobile, in 1922 Herb Hilman converted the front of the hotel to a Gulf service station and garage, which today is Wessel's auto repair.

After her husband's death in 1871, Mary Baehre opened a boarding house at the family home, located at 709 Franklin Street in Grand Haven. Mary's death came 62 years after her husband's. Boarding houses provided convenient quarters for transients and were a source of reliable income for indigent widows.

Development of the North Shore was the result of Harold Worm's vision and effort. His father built a log cabin there in 1927, and soon afterward, Harold constructed a two-story Tudor-style beachside home that remains in the family today. A concrete road from Ferrysburg to the Coast Guard Station was constructed in 1928.

In 1905, two Grand Rapids brewers, Jacob Veit and August Tusch, bought a parcel of land later known as Veit's Landing. Located on a point of land near Smith's Bayou in Ferrysburg, their cottages were almost hidden by the trees.

Two

LIFE SAVING SERVICE AND COAST GUARD

Fall storms on Lake Michigan are notoriously treacherous and in the early history of shipping, wrecks in and near Grand Haven harbor were common, often with substantial loss of life. To assist in saving lives, the United States Life Saving Service, a forerunner of the Coast Guard, was founded as a volunteer outfit in 1871.

The breeches buoy was a standard and critical part of the lifesaving process. The crewmen here are ready to practice shooting their line to a ship stranded on a sandbar. Once the line was secured, the crew of the imperiled ship could be brought to shore one at a time.

Grand Haven's first lifesaving station, built on the north side of the Channel, opened on May 1, 1877. The crew pictured here posed in front of their lifeboat in the early 1900s.

From 1856 to 1905, a masonry lighthouse on a high bluff above the Oval guided ships into Grand Haven harbor. The lighthouse's beacon, 150 feet above lake level, flashed regularly. The lighthouse keeper lived in the square building. Frank Fraga, shown with his wife, was lighthouse keeper from 1900 to 1911.

In 1905, the American Bridge Company erected a steel plate conical light tower to guide ships into port. The tower was 39 feet tall from base to parapet and 51 feet tall overall. The fog house, a rectangular frame structure, was sheathed with corrugated iron in 1922 to prevent deterioration. The catwalk allowed crews to reach the buildings during stormy conditions.

The first Coast Guard Community Picnic, planned for 1924, quickly became an annual event. In 1934, the first expanded picnic was held. By 1937, the Junior Chamber of Commerce staged the first Water Festival, which included three days of competitive races and drills. The Cutter *Escanaba* held open houses at each Festival until the start of World War II.

In August of 1934, the City of Grand Haven celebrated its 100th anniversary, and, incidentally, crowned its first queen. The young woman receiving the Miss Grand Haven crown from Mayor Lionel Heap was Esther De Witt. The annual custom of naming a Coast Guard Queen wouldn't start for another five years.

The early Coast Guard Festivals included training demonstrations, such as this one. Pictured here are the lifeboats in action in the Grand River Channel in 1937.

Jessie Olsen was crowned the first Coast Guard Festival Queen in 1939. She is standing behind the life preserver. Joining her on the boat are members of the court.

Taken in the 100 block of Washington, this photograph catches the local Coast Guard contingent marching in a World War II parade. Hill's Hardware, Boer's Furniture Store, and Hostetter's Newsstand are some of the businesses in the background.

In December of 1922, the Coast Guard abandoned its first headquarters and moved slightly down river to a larger frame structure. A four-stall marine garage was added in 1927. When the Coast Guard moved to the south side of the channel in 1989, the main building was converted to a private residence.

In 1915, an Act of Congress merged the Life Saving Service with the Revenue Cutter Service to form the United States Coast Guard. On a snowy December day in 1932, the newly commissioned Coast Guard Cutter *Escanaba* sailed for the first time into the port of Grand Haven.

The area's favorite ship, the *Escanaba*, went to war in March of 1942 and was destroyed while on convoy duty in the North Atlantic in 1943. Of the 103 crewmen aboard, only two were rescued.

Toward the end of World War II, the mast of the *Escanaba* was brought to Grand Haven, and in 1944 it was installed in Kelly Park. The name was changed to Escanaba Park in 1949.

The Cutter *Woodbine* steamed into port in 1947 as a replacement for the *Escanaba*. The ship remained in service until 1972, when it was followed by the tug *Raritan*. The barracks almost hidden behind the dunes once housed the men of the Civilian Conservation Corps. The brick building that housed municipal offices was turned over to the Coast Guard as Group Command Headquarters.

Three

INDUSTRIES

During the 19th century, as many as two dozen sawmills dotted the banks of the Grand River in and near Grand Haven. The mill owners provided room and board at places such as the Nortonville Boarding House, located several miles upriver and run by the Ottawa County Boom Company. Booming companies were responsible for collecting the logs and "herding" them to the sawmills.

Although the lumber industry in Northwest Ottawa County was essentially extinct by 1890, a few local sawmills continued to flourish. The one in this picture is not identified, but it may have belonged to Derk Vyn, who harvested timber from the Rosy Mound area.

The Silas Kilbourn Company used waste lumber to fashion a variety of wooden shipping boxes for fish, syrup, pickles, and cider. The company went out of business in 1910. Pictured, from left to right, are Burt Fant, an unidentified boy, Ralph Tripp, Henry Tysman, and another unidentified person.

Begun in 1874, the Boyden & Akeley Shingle Mill was, in its prime, the largest shingle mill in the world. At its peak, the company cut 937,000 shingles in 11 1/2 hours and in the same time period produced 100,000 board feet of lumber.

A good port and the availability of timber led naturally to the development of ship building. Established in 1867 by Thomas W. Kirby, John W. Callister, and John Neil, Mechanics Ship Yard and Dry Docks produced a variety of sail and propeller-driven boats, including the 1,460-ton steamer *H.C. Akeley*.

Employees of the Broom Factory proudly display some of their wares. Simple "parlor brooms" sold for $1.25 each wholesale. The company, which started in about 1885, advertised that it carried "All Kinds of Brooms and Brushes."

Ten employees of the Broom Company appear to have worked in rather cramped quarters, but the wood stove must have made the place cozy—perhaps too cozy with all that straw laying about.

Dwight Cutler and Hunter Savidge established the Cutler & Savidge Lumber Company in 1858. Located in the Village, the lumber yard stretched from the banks of Spring Lake to the foot of Division Street and west to the railroad bridge. Much of the ground in that area was composed of sawdust and cuttings.

Grand Haven Basket Factory opened for business in 1897 in a large frame structure on Grand Haven's north side. The average annual output was 150,000 berry crates, 1,500,000 peach baskets, 200,000 celery crates, and 360,000 baskets for smoked fish. The five men and a boy pictured here were ready for a break from their labors. The company ceased operations in 1925.

The H.J. Dornbos & Bros. Company started a commercial fish processing business in 1889. This picture of its headquarters at 614 Monroe Street in Grand Haven shows its founder, Henry Dornbos, dressed in a bow tie, and his brother, Gerrit, standing next to the horse toward the back.

The Dornbos fishing business became one of the largest and best-equipped fisheries in Michigan and became known nationwide for its smoked fish. In 1962, it was destroyed by a botulism epidemic, which was traced to a load of fish that sat on an unrefrigerated truck over the weekend.

In 1914, brothers Martin and Roy O'Beck of Grand Haven built one of the first steel tugboats in the area to use in their commercial fishing business. Martin is the man at the far right in this picture. The reels of netting were part of their fishing gear. An Interurban car is visible in the upper left.

Not all fish caught commercially were exported! Some were pedaled door-to-door from a fish wagon, such as the one shown here.

The Clinker Boat Company was organized in 1887 with William Barrett as Vice President. "Clinker" referred to boats in which external planks were attached so that the edge of one overlapped the next. When Barrett became sole owner of the firm, it was known as the Spring Lake Boat Company.

Johnston Boiler Works was founded in Ferrysburg in 1864 by John Watt Johnston. The company has successfully adapted to changing economies and technologies and endures today. Johnston boilers were used in construction of the Panama Canal in 1907, building the Mackinac Bridge in the mid-1950s, and production of pile-driving power for oil drilling platforms in recent years.

The nine men pictured in their executive offices at Challenge Corn Planter Co. are identified, from left to right, as Levi Scofield, Willard Sheldon, John Lockie, Frank Harbeck, Mr. Walsh, Mr. Borman, and Mr. Van Dongen. In addition to corn planters, the company also produced the Challenge Iceberg Refrigerator. Founded in 1883, the company ceased operations in 1929.

The Dake Engine Company, formed in Grand Haven in 1887, manufactured compact marine and stationary engines, particularly the double reciprocating square piston model. The Dake steam engine won a medal at the World Columbian Exposition in Chicago in 1893.

Perhaps as a demonstration of its power, the locally-produced Panhard truck appears to be towing a Grand Trunk locomotive. The trucks were produced in Grand Haven from 1917 to 1919. An unusual feature in those days was pneumatic tires, standard equipment on the front wheels.

Shortly after Keller Pneumatic Tool Company moved from Wisconsin to Grand Haven in 1917, the name was changed to William H. Keller, Inc., and in 1944, to the Keller Tool Co. It merged with Gardner-Denver in 1954. President William Keller is shown in this early photograph.

In 1904, Peter Van Zylen went into the lumber business under the name of Van Zylen Lumber Company. He dealt in lumber, sashes, doors and roofing. The company started business at the corner of Sixth and Adams Streets in Grand Haven, but later moved to the 400 block of Seventh.

In this interior view of Peter Van Zylen's Lumberyard the horse and wagon appear ready to take a load of materials to a building site.

The date and reason for this parade have been lost in time, but the brass band is ready to toot and the spectators are eager to march to the beat. The building in the background housed the Story & Clark Piano Factory offices. The company started manufacturing in Grand Haven in 1900.

This interior shot of the Story & Clark Piano Factory shows the workmen in the finishing department. It was a messy job, but a fine, enduring finish was critical to the completed product.

In 1906, the Board of Trade induced William Heap & Sons to move from Muskegon to Grand Haven. Heap began operations in 1907 at 1401 Fulton. The company manufactured plumbers' supplies made of wood.

Started in Chicago in 1865 as the Eagle Tanning Works, this company purchased the assets of the Grand Haven Leather Company and brought its manufacturing facility to the area in 1900. Today the company is known as Eagle Ottawa and continues to produce leather upholstery for automobiles.

This small building at the foot of Washington Street was erected in the 1890s to serve as the ticket office for Nat Robbins's Goodrich Steamship Line Agency. Ships sailed daily to Chicago, Milwaukee, and other Great Lakes ports. In about 1900, the fare for a round trip ticket to Chicago was $5.00, while a one-way ticket was $3.00.

Three generations of one Chicago family guided the destiny of Construction Aggregates Corporation from its start in Ferrysburg in 1907: Mandel Sensibar, the founder, and his descendants, Jacob, Ezra, and David.

Four

Downtowns

In this view, the camera looks east from the corner of Second and Washington Streets. The steeple of the First Reformed Church stands tall in the left center. The Akeley Building, soon to be home to the Tri-Cities Historical Museum, is in the right foreground.

Founded in 1834, Grand Haven quickly became a recreational, agricultural, and industrial center. Its downtown business district flourished, thanks in large part to the railway and ship lines. A portion of the railroad depot, now the site of the Tri-Cities Historical Museum, is visible at the left.

Despite parking meters and parallel parking, customers in the 1950s found downtown Grand Haven a good place to do their Christmas shopping, go to the bank, or see a movie. Built in 1916, the Robinhood Theater, which usually showed a mystery and a cowboy movie, was torn down in 1970.

Daniel Gale and John Pfaff's store at 114 Washington gave customers the chance to buy groceries and "Queen's Ware," a popular brand of glass products and earthenware dishes made in Britain. Also available were "Michigan Oil," apples, Royal Baking Powder, and kerosene lamps. The two owners pose with their wares in the 1878 photograph.

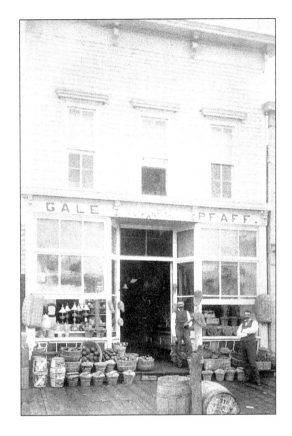

Around 1900, John Pfaff opened an insurance office in downtown Grand Haven. The older gentleman is Dwight Cutler, who built the magnificent Cutler House. Next to him is his son, Dwight Jr. Visible in the reflection of the window above the door is the spire of the Norris Hotel, located across the street.

In 1877, John J. Boer opened the Boer & Bolt grocery store in partnership with his future father-in-law, Henry Bolt, near the corner of Seventh and Washington Streets. Boer became better known for his furniture and undertaking store on Washington Street.

Around 1900, Enne Kraai opened a flour, feed, and grain store at 309 Fulton, where he and his wife resided. The building also doubled as a boarding house. In this photo, the cart and horse are ready to deliver bags of grain and a dog carefully guards the shipment. A poster in the store window advertises Ferry seeds.

Around 1853, Antoine Bottje erected a building to house his dry goods store. Bottje sold such things as flour, buttons, boots, thread, and whiskey. The whiskey sold for $1.25 a gallon, for which customers provided their own containers. Posing with him are two of his daughters.

In the early 1900s, the People's Mercantile Company was located on North Seventh Street in Grand Haven. The store offered groceries and dry goods. The sign in back advertises "Oleomargarine Sold Here."

Peter Van Lopik opened the Central Clothing House in downtown Grand Haven in the early 1900s and used his display windows to showcase the latest in fashionable menswear. Peter also manufactured the popular middy blouses for the girls at Akeley Institute.

Central Clothing offered men's suits, shirts, collars, shoes and a variety of accessories, as well as a staff of well-dressed clerks ready to assist their discriminating customers. In was open for business from the 1890s to the 1920s.

In 1889, at the age of 11, Gerrit Ekkens started working for his grandfather in the family general store. When the Van Lopiks dropped out of the business in 1907, Arie Van Toll joined Gerrit Ekkens and they continued under the name Van Toll & Ekkens. In 1913, Van Toll sold his interest in the store to Ekkens, and their partnership ended. Three of the Van Lopik brothers are pictured standing in the doorway.

From 1913 to 1953, Gerrit Ekkens, famous as Grand Haven's "Cheese King," was the sole owner of the grocery store at 206 Washington. Cheese was cured in the cellar and sold by mail throughout the country. Locally, Ekkens delivered his products with the horse and wagon shown here.

Prior to the fire of 1889, the magnificent Cutler House maintained a horse and carriage barn at the corner of Columbus and Third Streets. It was replaced by Stone's Livery and then, in the early 1900s, Dan Riley took over the business.

Spring Lake resident Thomas Savidge ran a livery and "Sale Stable" on Washington Street. The next building to the right housed Peter Dornbos's cigar-making and retail business. Savidge, standing in the wagon, appears to be taking a cartload of youngsters on a jaunt.

In 1908 the Grand Haven Baking Company on Washington Street advertised: "*Our Bakery Products are prepared in a clean, modern, sanitary bakery—a fact that is known to every resident of this community. An ever-increasing demand is an indisputable evidence that we produce 'good things to eat.'*"

You can almost smell the bread baking in the large ovens at the Grand Haven Bakery. Judging from the number of loaves on the rack, the bakery did a good business in the early 1900s.

This early 1920s picture was taken before the Grand Theater opened in 1928. The large building on the corner once housed John Boyink's saloon and then Mrs. Garnsey's Gift Shop and Tea Room. Many of the buildings were razed to make room for the Grand.

In 1927, construction began on the Grand Theater, Grand Haven's fifth and most ornate movie house. The "modern theatre" seated 833. The movie house opened to the public for the first time on Monday, January 23, 1928.

Gerrit Vanden Bosch founded a retail business at 100 North Third Street in 1875. At first, the store sold groceries and dry goods, and in 1884 a clothing department was added under the management of Thomas and Henry Vanden Bosch.

When Ed Baas of Grand Haven purchased the Vanden Bosch Store on Third Street in 1943, he was buying a business that already was almost 70 years old. Popularly known as the Big Store, it stayed in operation under Baas family management until late 1999.

Louis Fortino opened the Grand Haven Fruit Company on Washington Street in 1911. When fire destroyed the business in 1930, Louis moved to 114 Washington. A third generation of Fortinos now owns and manages the store, identified by the Royal Crown Cola sign in this picture.

Standing between Neal and Berdean Verhoek is Paul Fortino, son of business founder Louis Fortino. The Fortino store became known for a variety of specialty and imported items, particularly roasted peanuts.

Around 1900, Pine Street in Ferrysburg had plank sidewalks, street lamps, and small businesses like the Wielstedt Market, shown here with two clerks standing ready to welcome customers. Johnston Boiler Company is in the background.

This view looking west along Savidge Street in Spring Lake shows Campbell's Drug Store on the corner. Just up the street is the Home Restaurant and Spring Lake State Bank. The three-story building with the Crescent Flour ad is still standing, but the top floor has been removed.

Braak's Bakery

In 1903, Jacob Braak and Hendrik K. Bulthuis started Spring Lake Bakery at 110 West Savidge. It was later known as Braak's Bakery. Jacob composed the secret recipe for "Town Talk" cookies, which he preferred to cut by hand. The cookies became a local favorite.

This frame building's long history as a grocery store and meat market began with Noah Perkins, who erected it in the late 1850s. After the Civil War, Henry Millard bought the building from Perkins's widow and started his own grocery. The building was eventually razed.

In 1877, Ormond Messinger sold his furniture store to Henry Cliff and opened a stationery and drug business at 208 West Savidge Street in Spring Lake. A sign in the window announced that the store was an agent for White Laundry in Grand Haven.

In the 1880s, John Perham owned a dry goods store on Savidge Street in Spring Lake. Judge Allan Adsit was initially his partner, but sold out to Perham eight years after opening. Perham is standing in the doorway of his store. Martha Reenders is the woman to his left.

The Spring Lake State Bank, which opened at 304 West Savidge in 1914, was relocated to a new building at 210 West Savidge in 1918. The Michigan State Police occupied the second floor. In 1954, the bank moved to the northwest corner of Buchanan and Savidge Streets.

An 1871 fire destroyed much of Spring Lake Village, including Aloys Bilz's businesses. He immediately rebuilt and continued to sell stoves, hardware, farm implements, and furniture. He also had an insurance and real estate business within this block of buildings on Savidge Street.

Five

SERVICES, PRIVATE AND PUBLIC

In the early years of settlement, county business was transacted on the second floor of Henry Griffith's drugstore on the northwest corner of Washington and First Streets. The two-story frame building pictured here served as the County Court House beginning in 1857. That structure was purchased by the Christian School in 1893 for $248 and moved to 800 Columbus.

The early fire departments were made up of volunteers. Shown here is the Hunter Savidge Fire Company in the Village of Spring Lake. They were in action by the early 1870s, about the same time as the Village Fire Department. The Exchange Street School, built in 1869, can be seen through the tree leaves on the right.

In 1898, the Grand Haven Fire Department purchased two horses to draw the fire wagon and displayed them proudly in front of the department garage for this photograph. The animals grazed across the street in the new Central Park. The Department bought its first motorized vehicle more than 20 years later. The 1894 County Building is visible in the background.

Proud Grand Haven firefighters pose in front of their new 33-foot American-La France fire engine just after it was purchased in 1942. Powered by a 12-cylinder engine, it could pump 750 gallons of water a minute. The truck carried as many as 15 firefighters at a time, most of them hanging on to the truck's side. The truck served local firefighting needs for 32 years.

Searles Vandenberg was one of the first Sheriff's deputies in Ottawa County to use a motorcycle in his law enforcement duties. Searles, who was born in 1907, appears to be in his 20s in this photo.

The growing popularity of automobiles necessitated hard-surface roads for travel, a special treat in wet weather. Workers in this photograph, taken around 1910, survey the task of laying a concrete curb and gutter on Fulton Street, between Fifth and Sixth Streets. Streets usually were paved with brick.

Concrete sidewalks were laid before the streets were paved. In some cases, the concrete walks replaced wooden platforms. The neighborhood in this picture is unidentified, but the workmen were clearly ready for a photo-op.

The purpose of the work being done here isn't recorded, but clearly it took the labor of many—and some ingenuity—to raise the pole into position. Although concrete had replaced wood plank sidewalks, Washington Street was not yet paved with brick, an improvement that came in 1910.

The Grand Haven Water Works provided running water for fire hydrants in 1882. Called the Wiley Water Works, the brick structure was located at 1510 Washington. Six years later, the City of Grand Haven took over the system and moved the water works to a building at Clinton and Harbor. Residential water came soon afterward.

The area's first telephone exchange was installed by Thomas Parish in 1881 with 20 subscribers. At first, wires were strung from almost any convenient spot above ground, including rooftops and tree branches. The innovation was a source of curiosity and people would line up at a telephone to find out if it worked.

Horrace Nichols, who owned the *Grand Haven Courier Journal*, purchased the *Grand Haven Daily Tribune* in 1891 and continued as owner-publisher until 1915. Nichols, the bearded gentleman in this 1910 picture, is accompanied by Kate Pipple at the far left. Kingsbury Scott and Mary De Young are seated between them.

Grand Haven's first post office was located in the Ferry warehouse on the waterfront. In 1872, the town's first post office building was erected at the corner of Washington and First Streets, a structure that remains in use today. The post office remained in this building until 1905, when a new "Federal Building" was put up on the northwest corner of Washington and Third Streets.

Grand Haven's post office was a hub of activity, a place where townspeople gathered to catch up on gossip, find out about upcoming events, and to see if they had received any long awaited letters or parcels. Upon the inception of rural mail delivery, shortly after the turn of the century, the 1872 post office became a much quieter place.

Parked on the brick street in front of the Armory, this phaeton was festooned with flags for a tour of the city that would instill patriotism and sell war bonds to a supportive public. Accompanying Walter Boyd, the driver, were Bill Wilds, Bud Vyn, Bill Baker, and Captain Dykema. The automobile was manufactured in Muskegon.

Uzell B. Eames was named the first Postmaster in Ferrysburg in 1859. Throughout the 1860s and 1870s, the Ferrysburg Post Office was housed in a general store. During the next decade, Eames erected a one-room frame building on the west side of Pine Street to function as the Post Office. In about 1897, the building was moved across the street to Johnston Boiler property to better serve the company's needs.

In 1939, a camp for Civilian Conservation Corps workers opened in Mulligan's Hollow, later the site of the YMCA. The CCC was a nationwide depression-era organization developed to prevent an excess of topsoil loss due to erosion. The CCC accomplished its mission by laying brush on sand blows and planting dune grass and pine trees to stop or retard the movement of sand.

In 1879, about 40 local men organized an independent military company that came to be known as Company F. During the Spanish-American War, Company F served as part of the United States Infantry. The men saw no action, but returned to Grand Haven as heroes. The group gathered under their Welcome Home sign at the corner of Washington and Second Streets.

Early on, physicians saw the advantage of visiting patients in a car rather than using a horse and carriage. Dr. Cyril Brown of Spring Lake was one of the first in this area to have his own automobile, a Sears Roebuck make. The doctor's house at 223 East Savidge is behind him.

Dr. Peter vanden Berg returned to his birthplace, Grand Haven, in about 1910 to serve as Health Officer. Vanden Berg died at his home at 219 South Fifth on March 2, 1921. From the looks of his shelves in this picture, he carried a good supply of pharmaceuticals.

Once the home of Captain William Loutit and his family, this two-story frame house on Fifth Street was converted into the area's first hospital in 1919. It was made possible through the generosity of William Hatton, who named it the Elizabeth Hatton Memorial Hospital in honor of his deceased wife. Many years later, the structure was demolished and replaced by the Presbyterian Church Sunday School.

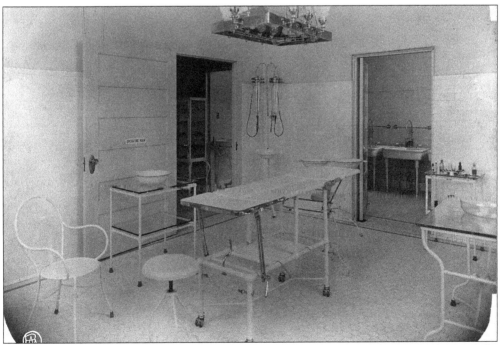

The first operation performed at Hatton Memorial Hospital was a tonsillectomy. The first baby delivered in the new hospital was Elizabeth Vyn Meier, born on July 4, 1919. The operating room is shown in this picture.

The area's second hospital was built in 1939 at a cost of $76,915. The two-and-a-half-story brick building had a capacity of 47 beds and a staff of 10 physicians. The first floor was for medical-surgical patients, and the second floor housed obstetrics, the operating room, and a delivery suite.

A generous bequest in 1922 made it possible for the Salvation Army to purchase the "Grey Block" at 16 Washington. The organization used the building as its headquarters until moving to a new site in 1975.

Undoubtedly dressed in their finest, this group of Spring Lake students poses in front of the school. A few of them may have presented their teacher with the potted plants displayed on the windowsill.

Starting in 1888, Akeley Institute for Girls provided educational opportunities for young women and cultural programs for the entire community. Located across the street from Central Park, the tree-lined campus had many stately buildings for classes and dormitories. The last class graduated in 1928.

Grand Haven's first Central School was constructed on a high crest near the corner of Sixth and Franklin Streets. It provided instruction for grades five through twelve. When classes began in 1871, there were 11 teachers in 11 classrooms. The school's first graduating class, in 1876, had three students. The building was destroyed by fire in 1901.

High school students moved from the old Central School on Sixth Street to this new brick building on Seventh Street in 1922. In 1953, another high school was built near the south end of Seventh Street. The Seventh Street school was then used as a junior high school, and was razed in 1967 when a newer junior high opened on Griffin Street.

About 40 Grand Haven men organized themselves into the "Yates Light Infantry" in April, 1879. When the group was appointed for state service, they assembled as Company F, Second Regiment of the Michigan State Troops. Although part of the state militia, Company F was a stock company and financed entirely by local "investors."

Over the years, the members of Company F served in the Spanish-American War and World Wars I and II. It also assisted the State of Michigan in keeping the peace during various trouble spots. This 1942 picture shows World War II army inductees boarding buses that will take them to boot camp.

After meeting many years at the "community building" on Second Street, the congregation of the Grand Haven Presbyterian Church constructed a new place of worship in the 200 block of Washington in 1855. Thirty years later, the church edifice, without porch or vestibule, was moved to the corner of Franklin and Fifth Streets, as pictured here.

St. Mary's, the church closest to the camera and well-hidden by a clump of tall trees, was built on North Division Street in Spring Lake in 1857. Just beyond it was another church, constructed in 1882 by thirty-five families who were tired of making the journey into Grand Haven every Sunday. They called their new place the Holland Christian Reformed Church.

In 1870, members of the First Reformed Church dedicated their third place of worship, pictured here. It was lost to fire in the 1889 conflagration. The congregation replaced the building the next year, but its lifetime proved to be even shorter as it burned to the ground on June 8, 1907.

During the 1940s and 1950s, the Women's Club hosted the Summer Stock Theater, a precursor to the Central Park Players. The Unitarian Church built the structure in 1888. Upon formation in 1891, the Women's Club started meeting in the two-story frame building, and acquired it in 1924. It was razed to make room for the post office in 1966.

The Carnegie Public Library was built on North Third Street in 1913, and remained the city library until a new one was built at 407 Columbus in 1965. Two years later the original library was torn down to secure parking space for a bank.

Organized in May 1959, the Tri-Cities Historical Society arranged exhibits in the display windows of downtown businesses, such as this 1959 layout at the Reichardt shop. Three years later, the Masons provided permanent exhibit space on the second floor of their building at 222 Washington.

Six
RESIDENCES, HUMBLE AND GRAND

This lovely residence, the home of Leroy and Susannah Heath and their family, was located on East Savidge Street in Spring Lake. The cow and windmill behind the house convey a sense of everyday life in the 1800s. Two bird cages are suspended from the ceiling of the side porch.

Hunter Savidge built this home on Mason Street in Spring Lake in 1857, where it stayed until it was moved to Barber Street. Savidge gave the house to Jay McCluer as partial payment for substituting for him in the Civil War, a common practice at that time. When McCluer relocated to 301 Barber about 1885, his son Marshall moved into the home on Mason.

In 1871, Hunter Savidge built this majestic home for his family on Park Street in Spring Lake. At that time, the property encompassed the entire block. When Catherine and William Loutit returned to the Tri-Cities area in 1948, they made their home at this address. It was razed in 1967.

The frame house at 316 East Savidge in Spring Lake was built prior to 1869. The Shoemaker family moved into it in 1883. John L. Shoemaker, a descendant of the original owner, moved into the home in 1919 with his wife, Lena. Many years later, it was purchased by Christ Community Church and converted to apartments.

In 1872, after a destructive fire, Aloy Bilz of Spring Lake rebuilt his residence on its original Division Street site. Constructed of white pine, it had nine-foot cathedral windows with movable interior and exterior shutters. The house featured two fireplaces, 12-foot ceilings, and wood plank floors. In 1908, electricity was installed, and plumbing was added in 1912.

The Soule home at the southeast corner of Barber and Division Streets in the Village of Spring Lake was built prior to 1864. Judging from the bicycle leaning against the fence, the picture dates to about 1910. Heavy "eyebrows" over the numerous windows give the home a distinctive look. It was destroyed by fire a number of years ago.

Located on North Park Street, the Joseph and Lucy Finch home was built in 1858, making it one of the earliest permanent residences in Spring Lake. Lucy, who died in 1912, outlived her husband by more than 20 years.

Spring Lake resident Robert Loosemoore worked as a sawyer at one of the nearby mills. He died in Spring Lake in 1918, ten years after his wife, Phidelia. The house burned down in April, 1956.

In the early 1900s, the Thum family of Grand Rapids had a 36-acre summer residence, complete with a boathouse, on Spring Lake. The Thums had made a substantial fortune by perfecting and producing "Tanglefoot Sticky Fly Paper." In 1931, the Spring Lake Yacht Club negotiated for a long-term lease on the Thums' property, and has remained there ever since.

Dick Bolt operated a meat market on North Seventh Street in Grand Haven. He and his wife lived in the house next door, as shown in this picture. His shop is just visible at the left. Bolt died in 1938.

William and Fanny Harper built this house on South Second Street in the early 1870s. At that time, the hill was so steep that even pedestrians negotiated it with difficulty. The Harpers occupied the home for more than two years before teams of horses could ascend Second Street hill from the north. It was only when the city laid a plank road that it really became a street.

In about 1855, Thomas White built a house at the corner of Columbus and First Streets in Grand Haven. His nephew, U. S. Senator Thomas White Ferry, occupied the home, which was rimmed by a wide lawn, shaded by tall maple trees, and graced with a variety of plants. Inside, the den was filled with mementos of the Senator's life of public service.

This gabled home, reminiscent of the Gothic style, was built at 401 Sheldon Road, at the junction of Fifth, Pennoyer, Howard, and Sheldon. It was the residence of Dr. Enoch Cummings, a Grand Haven dentist. Cummings evidently lived here before building the large home at 482 Sheldon Terrace. In later years, the house was converted to a duplex.

John and Sarah Stark lived in this house at 232 Franklin, on the corner of Third and Franklin Streets in Grand Haven, around 1900. The yard is rimmed with wooden plank sidewalks. Their daughter, Margaret, was the first librarian of record in Grand Haven. John Stark, a marine engineer, died in 1903.

The home at 215 South Fourth Street was the residence of Jurrien and Dirkje Ball. Jurrien owned a dry goods store on Washington Street for 41 years. Built by the couple in 1880, the home was neither grandiose nor elaborate, but a conservative house which was inhabited by unpretentious people.

The lumber industry made fortunes for many and led to the construction of several magnificent homes. One of them was the Boyden House on Fifth Street. Built in 1871 by Charles Boyden, the home was marked by the gambrel-style roof, indicative of the Dutch Colonial style. Perhaps the girls stopped by on their bike ride to admire its many features. It is now a bed and breakfast.

The two-story frame house at 221 South Seventh Street was built in 1884. John J. and Anna Danhof raised their four children here. The wrap-around porch, visible today, was a later addition. The house was not far from the homes of John's brother, James Danhof, and a cousin, Peter Danhof, both of whom lived around the corner on Lafayette.

The home of Great Lakes sea captain William R. Loutit was built at the northwest corner of Washington and Fourth Streets in 1894. W.A. Nethercot of Austin, Illinois, was the architect. The home had large rooms with high ceilings, multiple fireplaces, a ballroom, game room, and living quarters for the servants. It was carpeted throughout. The structure was torn down about 1959.

Dwight Cutler and his wife lived in this residence at the southeast corner of Washington and Third Streets. After it was destroyed in the great fire of October 1889, they built the magnificent home pictured here. The estate included a carriage house and stables. A community leader, Cutler built the magnificent hotel on the opposite corner that bore the family name, which also was lost in the 1889 fire.

This house on Fulton Street was the residence of Arend J. Nyland and his family in the 1890s. Behind the house was an open field leading to the river. At that time, Fulton was unpaved and a plank sidewalk lined the street. Nyland became President of the Grand Haven Leather Company, later known as Eagle Ottawa.

The *May Graham* plied the Grand River for decades. It was retired in 1918 and its pilot house was placed on the north side of the Grand River, at the future site of the North Shore Marina, to serve as a cottage. When the marina was constructed in 1952, the cabin was relocated, this time to a site on Pottawatomie Bayou in Grand Haven Township, where it continues to serve as a cottage.

In 1898, Nathaniel Robbins built this home on the corner of Fifth and Franklin for his wife, Esther Savidge, at an extravagant cost of $25,000. The main floor had four large rooms, a kitchen, and two baths. The second floor contained five bedrooms and three of the home's seven baths. A large ballroom filled the third floor.

Known as "the Castle," this brick structure high atop Five Mile Hill was constructed in 1928 to resemble a 15th century Spanish castle. The brick was imported from Italy. At different times in the 1950s and 1960s, the Castle served as a restaurant, nightclub, and pizza place. More recently, the 6,000 square foot structure was converted into a bed and breakfast.

Seven
Transportation Over Land and On Water

By the early 1900s, manufacturing businesses were identifying Grand Haven as an excellent spot to build new plants and attract willing workers. This view, taken from Dewey Hill, provides a clear image of the Story & Clark Piano Company, which started production in 1900. Its first two buildings are visible just beyond the ship moored in the foreground.

The railroad made its way to the mouth of the Grand River in 1858, staying on the north side of the river in order to avoid the expense of building a bridge. A depot, a hotel, restaurants, and small businesses soon developed at the foot of Dewey Hill. Passengers and freight were ferried across the river. Twelve years later, a bridge was built and the railroad came directly into Grand Haven.

This 1868 photograph of Grand Haven, taken from the crest of Dewey Hill, provides a glimpse of the Ferry & Son Building on Harbor Drive, the Kirby House at the foot of Washington, the Presbyterian Church in the 200 block of Washington, the two-story frame County Court House farther up the street, and Central School on Sixth Street, which was then considered the outskirts of the growing village.

The *William H. Barrett*, a well-known river and lake vessel, was launched in 1874. The 75 cent fare from Eastmanville to Grand Haven included one meal. The *Barrett* was known for causing a fire that destroyed much of the east side of Spring Lake in 1893. Here the packet is entering Grand Haven harbor. The waterfront's second lighthouse is the white building on the sand dune.

On the other side of the Grand River, the dock and ferry that connected 144th Street in Spring Lake and Robinson Townships are barely visible. Puffing upriver is the packet *May Graham*, undoubtedly carrying a load of passengers and mail to Grand Rapids and points between.

Built in 1872 at the Roberston Shipyard in Grand Haven, the two-masted schooner *City of Grand Haven* transported freight until 1923. Here it is moored on the west bank of the Channel.

This large ship is preparing to dock at the Washington Street Landing, where it will unload its passengers and wait to depart to "Milwaukee and All Points West." The tower, adjacent to the Grand Truck Railway Depot, housed the ticket office and waiting room for the Crosby Line ships.

The person standing near the starboard bow of the Goodrich steamer *Alabama* puts the size of the ship in perspective. The steamer carried passengers from 1912 through 1932. In its first year of operation, round trip fare between Chicago and Grand Haven was $3.50.

The development of Grand Haven as resort area led to a substantial increase in the number of passenger and freight ships visiting the port. By 1870, the railroad had moved from the north side of the Grand River to a depot near downtown Grand Haven. Part of the new depot is just visible in the lower right corner of this picture. The depot now houses the Tri-Cities Historical Museum.

Railroads could save hours of time and hundreds of miles of travel by shipping their cars across Lake Michigan between Grand Haven and Milwaukee. Beginning in 1903, entire trains were loaded into large ferry boats like this one to make the 75-mile trip across the lake, so that they could resume their iron path on the other side of the water.

Ice floes were dangerous to shipping enterprises, and also made entry into port something of a challenge. Spectators on the catwalk have a special view of four large ships as they attempt to enter Grand Haven harbor.

Ice was the enemy of all the ships, including the commercial fishing boats. Here the fishing tug *H.J. Dornbos* appears to have met its match in a dense ice jam.

This early 1900s view of Government Basin and Grand Haven Harbor puts area waterways in a broad perspective. On the left are a few of the fishing shanties nestled at the bottom of Dewey Hill. The tall structure in the back center is the grain elevator, part of the skyline for many years. The Corps of Army Engineers had the responsibility of keeping the fine harbor open for shipping.

Nat Brown and his remarkable camera on a kite caught this scene on January 10, 1912. Struggling to get out of the ice-jammed harbor were the *Alabama*, *Crosby*, *Nyack*, *Conestoga*, and two Grand Trunk car ferries, *Grand Haven* and *Milwaukee*.

An extensive network of rivers and lakes provided natural pathways for the transportation of people, freight, and mail. Jay McCluer, a Spring Lake resident, had the Robertson Shipyard build the *Lizzie Walsh* in 1884. McCluer and his sons operated it as a passenger boat to service cottages and resorts on Spring Lake.

The *City of Grand Rapids*, a two-decked stern-wheeler, was constructed at the Callister Ship Yard in Grand Haven. It was one of the larger intercity vessels to ply the area's waterways.

The last passenger train departed from the Grand Trunk Depot at the foot of Washington Street in 1958. Prior to that, the grounds near the waterfront were busy with passenger and freight trains entering and leaving the lakefront port. This early photo of the Grand Trunk engine and coal tender also shows the seven-story grain elevator on the banks of the Grand River in the background.

In Spring Lake, the Grand Trunk Western Railway Depot and Railway Express offices were located 504 West Savidge. The first train came through in 1858 and the last rumbled out of town in 1957. The depot was moved and now serves as an antique outlet.

In 1895, a group of local investors started the Grand Haven Street Railway Company. The railway used steam-powered engines to transport passengers from downtown Grand Haven out to the lakefront and Highland Park. It was called the "dummy line" because the engines didn't generate their own power, but picked up "charges" of steam at two points along the route.

The Interurban brought resorters to Highland Park over a wide expanse of sand. The majestic Highland Park Hotel sits high upon the sandy bluff in the center of the picture. The large frame building on the beach was later named Hyland Gardens and rotated to sit parallel to the beach.

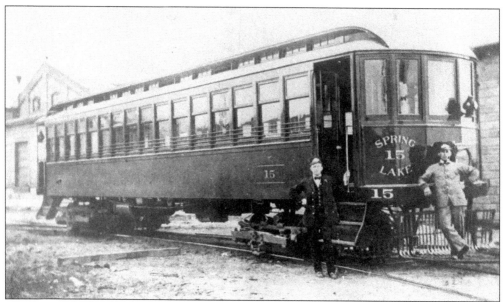

The Grand Haven Street Railway Company, formed in 1895, carried people from downtown to Highland Park and points of interest along the waterfront. A few years later, people as far away as Grand Rapids were able to make a quick, inexpensive journey to Spring Lake, Ferrysburg, Grand Haven, and the Lake Michigan beach.

For several decades in the early part of the 20th century, new automobiles were brought to Grand Haven, loaded on large freighters, and shipped across Lake Michigan. In this photo, the cars are lined up on Washington Street, ready for their voyage across the lake.

The bus pictured here, owned by George vanden Berg in the early 1920s, toured Washington Street and took passengers as far as Highland Park by way of Lake Avenue.

Begun by Derk Vyn as a "one-horse draying business" in 1857, Vyn Brothers Storage and Transfer Company later was located at the northwest corner of Third and Fulton Streets. Eventually Derk's sons took over the business. The brothers bought their first motorized vehicle in 1912 and by 1925 the company operated one of the largest fleets of trucks in the state.

This group of young people out for a tour could count on plenty of fresh air in their 4-door phaeton. The license plate is dated 1913. Behind them is the Highland Park Hotel.

Harry Potter anticipated the impact of the automobile during the early years of its industrial growth. As early as 1919, he opened a garage for the repair of trucks and cars on West Savidge Street in Spring Lake. He also offered Red Crown gasoline, tires, and "free air." Potter offered similar services on Franklin Street in Grand Haven.

Robert Barrett of Spring Lake has his bobsled loaded with children ready to go dashing through the snow. Robert, the son of William Barrett, eventually took over the management of his father's business, Spring Lake Boat Company, which was earlier known as the Clinker Boat Company.

The Ferrysburg train station was located near the foot of the railroad bridge that was built across the Grand River in 1870. The depot served both the Grand Trunk and Pere Marquette lines.

The Italianate-style Grand Trunk Depot at the foot of Washington Street featured semicircular arched windows, regularly spaced brick pilasters, and large, decorative brackets for the wide eaves. In time, the charm of the railroads declined, and in 1958 the last passenger train left the depot. In 1972, the Tri-Cities Historical Museum started using the depot for exhibits and office space.

Built in 1866, the area's first bridge over the Grand River in this area linked Spring Lake and Grand Haven. A second span, constructed in 1923, stretched from the north end of Seventh Street to Ferrysburg. Thirty years later, as part of the rerouting and general improvement of U.S. Hwy. 31, it was replaced by the drawbridge shown here. The railroad bridge was built in 1870.

Eight
Recreation and Leisure

It was not only the big lake that attracted swimmers. Spring Lake, rivers, and bayous were equally refreshing and provided an opportunity for family and friends to display the latest in swimwear fashion.

In 1916, Nat Robbins opened the first theater built expressly for showing motion pictures. Called the Robinhood, it was located at 217 Washington in downtown Grand Haven. It also could accommodate vaudeville skits and other traveling shows.

In the mid-1920s, a large warehouse owned by Nat Robbins was converted to a skating, dancing, and amusement center. Called "The Barn," it was located on South Harbor Drive. Louis C. Voelker and his wife had a refreshment stand where they served cherry cokes, tin-roof sundaes, and other treats. On April 25, 1946, a fire destroyed the Barn.

Spring Lake Country Club was founded in 1911 by William Savidge and other community leaders, after they purchased 140 acres of the Benjamin Soule farm for $6,000. A nine-hole golf course was laid out and the old farm home was converted into a clubhouse by bringing the dining room to the front of the house, while the barn became the men's locker and shower room.

The Country Club was a success. Growing membership soon made it necessary to expand the facilities, and in 1925 the organization issued bonds for the construction of a Spanish-style clubhouse. Caddies continued to use the old farmhouse for several more years.

In the early years of the Spring Lake Country Club, the many men and women who walked along, laden with lunch baskets, created a well-worn path between the far corner of the grounds and the clubhouse. As more men and women took up the sport, membership grew rapidly, and soon made it necessary to add a second round of nine holes.

Sailing on Spring Lake has been an important sport since the end of the 19th century, when the Spring Lake Yacht Club was founded. The Club sponsored regattas that allowed weekend sailors to display the trim lines and speed of their boats, as well as their seamanship. The Club's boathouse, pictured here, was destroyed by high water in 1952.

Baseball teams were organized in the Grand Haven area as early as the 1880s. In 1913, the Grand Haven Athletic Park was located near the corner of Sheldon and Taylor, now the site of North Ottawa Community Hospital. Among Grand Haven's team members were Jimmie Hine, "Crab" Pfaff, Carl Shaw, Jack Martin, Jake Van Dyke and "Babe" Woldring.

Although not in uniform, these men are members of an unidentified early 1900s baseball team and wear their gloves to show it. A bucket, casually placed near the bat, may have contained a few baseballs.

These eleven young men constituted Grand Haven High School's second football team. The inaugural team played its first game on November 23, 1895, and lost to Muskegon, 8–6. The team's average age was 16 and their average weight was a trim 134 pounds. The contests took place at Recreation Field, on the south side of Washington Street in the 1300 block.

Long before Title IX mandated it, Grand Haven Schools offered competitive sports for girls. In 1916 the girls' basketball team won all seven of its games, one by a score of 26 to 2. The final game of the season was played against their "old time rivals," Holland. The Blue and Gold of Grand Haven was victorious by a score of 17 to 8.

The hill on Second Street between Franklin and Lafayette beckoned youngsters to hop on the bob-sled and zip down the steep incline. Streets below were blocked off, and legend says that the sledders could make it all the way to the river, several blocks north.

Some of the youngsters brought their own sleds to make the icy trip down Second Street. Here they are lined up and ready to go!

The fish must have been biting on the peaceful day in 1940 when this picture was taken on the south pier. Many a cane pole is stretched toward the calm water, hoping to snag a perch or other pan fish for a delicious supper.

Before 1900, sport fishing took its place alongside commercial fishing as an important local activity. Anglers could fish off either pier with great success, or take a boat farther out into the lake to catch big ones like this sturgeon—the one that didn't get away.

Sailing on Spring Lake has been an important sport since the end of the 19th century. Boats small and large often entered regattas to show off their trim lines and speed.

Weekend sailors often displayed their boats and formed their own yacht clubs, as this group did at Arbutus Banks, which was a resort on the east shore of Spring Lake.

Bands, marchers, bikes, spectators, and downtown America. They all come together in this early 1900s view of Tony Pippel leading the Grand Haven Concert Band down the 100 block of Washington Street.

Andrew Thomson organized and directed the first local high school music ensemble. Known as the "Jackie Band," the name derived from the uniforms the young men wore, similar to that of the Navy Bluejackets. The group played concerts and parades throughout Michigan from 1915 to 1924.

The 90-room Pines Resort, located on the west shore of Spring Lake, was built in 1895. The grounds, amply shaded by the tall, white pines, gave the place its well-deserved name. Spacious houses provided comfortable quarters for guests, and it had a dock for the boats that brought passengers, mail, and supplies. Among other recreational activities, the Pines offered tennis.

Thomas John Kiel and Nellie J. Kermode were married in Grand Haven on June 6, 1901. They apparently made their honeymoon trip in this carriage, festooned with noise makers and a sign announcing the event.

Located on the north side of the channel, the world-famous and ever-popular Musical Fountain has played music on every summer day since 1963. Sometimes referred to as the "Dancing Waters," the fountain has also played an important part in the annual Coast Guard Festival Fireworks Show.

On December 2, 1964, one year after the inaugural run of the Musical Fountain, the traditional nativity scene made its first appearance on Dewey Hill. Michigan's Governor Romney presided over the festivities, which included a candle-lit parade, a choir, speeches, and a magic switch triggered by the Governor to illuminate the impressive scene.

In the original town plat, a block of land on the east boundary of Grand Haven was designated as the cemetery. By the end of the 19th century, the town's growth made it clear that the cemetery had to be moved. Graves were relocated to Lake Forest Cemetery, and the block of land was dedicated as Central Park in July, 1901.

Young Ivan Fosheim might have had a difficult time deciding which was more impressive, his up-to-date pedal car or the brass cannon from the War of 1812, then on display in Central Park. Akeley Institute is visible in the background.

The local Red Cross chapter created a special float to help celebrate Armistice Day in 1919. The Red Cross Ottawa County Chapter was founded in Grand Haven in 1908, only one of two chapters to exist in all of Michigan at that time.

There's always time for a snooze! Martin O'Beck, pictured here, may have had a hard day's fishing. In any event, he found an empty bin and put it to good use. His faithful friend kept an alert eye out for intruders who might interrupt his master's nap. Martin and his brother Roy followed in their father's footsteps and took up business in the commercial fishing industry.

Nine
DISASTERS, LARGE AND SMALL

On a dry, windy day in May of 1893 sparks from a riverboat ignited a fire that destroyed the Spring Lake schoolhouse, two churches, and 62 other buildings. Mary Loosemoore, who arrived on the scene via horse and cart, sits on the foundation to survey the damage. At the far right stands the Presbyterian Church, unscathed. The Wooley/Barrett home is in the left background.

It has been said that there were as many saloons as churches in the Grand Haven area—and there were a lot of churches! One of them, the First Reformed Church, burned to the ground three times at the same location. The fire shown here, which destroyed the congregation's second building, occurred in 1907. The newly-built post office across the street was saved from damage, but the church was a total loss. Its replacement burned down six years later.

Before moving to a new building on Second Street in 1948, the Fraternal Order of Eagles met on the second floor of 212 Washington. Their offices appear to be the location of the fire in this picture. Just to the right of the fire is James Vander Zalm's "Cheap Cash Department Store," where Jonker Hardware was later located.

After Grand Haven's first Central School burned down in 1901, it was rebuilt on the same site with a three-story masonry structure, also called Central School. It went up in flames in December of 1963. This building, too, was replaced, on a smaller scale, and became Central Elementary School for grades kindergarten through six.

Tragedy struck on Thanksgiving Day, 1902, when the Opera House on Second Street was devoured by flames. The destruction of the local landmark was pointedly sorrowful for the town because so many eminent artists had performed there, and it had served as headquarters for the local militia group called Company F since 1881.

Supported entirely by local subscription, members of Company F rebuilt their headquarters at 15 South Second Street in 1905. Called the Armory, the structure still stands at the start of the 21st century. The company was able to resume its drills in short time. Company F merged with the 32nd "Red Arrow" division for World War I combat.

The last major shipwreck off Grand Haven occurred in December of 1939, when the freighter *Sensibar* was being towed from Chicago to Grand Haven. The Coast Guard saved the crew by running out a breeches buoy to the freighter. No lives were lost.

While on its way from Grand Haven to Milwaukee in 1907, the steamer *Naomi* caught fire in the middle of Lake Michigan, threatening the lives of its 85 passengers and crew. Six people were killed in the disaster. The *Kansas*, a sister ship to the Naomi, towed the hulk into Grand Haven harbor. The wreck was rebuilt and served another 22 years.

Bitter cold and heavy snow marked the months of January and February, 1936. Snow banks became so high that keeping streets open was a challenge, and sometimes the byways looked more like canyons.

A series of powerful storms and an unrelenting cold snap during the winter of 1935 and 1936 created some impressive mountains of snow. Dated February 1936, this view looks west from the 100 block of Savidge. The store owners had done their part in clearing the sidewalks, but where did the cars park?

Caught in mid-flight by an alert photographer, the steeple flying through the air once adorned the Congregational Church at the corner of Sixth and Washington Streets. As a demolition crew attempted to remove the steeple, a large section of it flew through the air and became embedded in the ground.

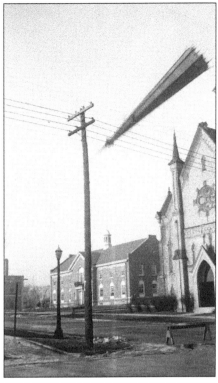

Airplanes also presented some peril to local citizens. In 1931, a small plane crashed into the house at 8 Clinton Street in Grand Haven. No one was killed, but the house certainly suffered.

Most of the time, the Interurban was a safe mode of travel, but occasionally a car would slide off the track, as it seems to have done on this snowy day near the intersection of Washington and Harbor.

The Grand Trunk locomotive is barely discernible in this terrible wreck that occurred near Nunica in the early 1900s, evidently the result of a head-on collision.

Visit us at
arcadiapublishing.com

CPSIA information can be obtained
at www.ICGtesting.com
Printed in the USA
LVHW061333301221
707548LV00003B/232